I LOVE YOU

LETTERS OF LOVE FROM
BLACK MEN TO BLACK BOYS

To help build their self-esteem & self-efficacy

NATE EVANS JR.

"We aren't raising boys,
we are building men."

DEDICATION

This book is dedicated to every black boy and black man who has ever felt unheard, worthless, misunderstood, and unloved. I want you to know that each author in this book loves you unconditionally and is rooting for you.

As black males, there is a stigma for us to be tough and never show our emotions. We are taught to believe that real strength comes from this behavior, but the reality is, that is weakness disguised as strength.

Real strength occurs when we are willing to be vulnerable. Real strength comes from admitting where we are weak. Real strength comes from God.

"Do I matter, is my voice being heard?

On June 8ᵗʰ, 2019, I attended the "Can We Talk" Conference in Washington, D.C. which was hosted by award-winning actress Taraji P. Henson. My mission with attending this conference as someone who was not a licensed mental health professional was to learn more about the state of mental health in the black community.

At the time, I was a student at Rowan University, and I was completing my bachelor's degree. I remember that there was a point at the conference when I was sitting at a table during brunch with my fiancée, who is a licensed social worker, and we were accompanied by a licensed therapist, and also a brain surgeon.

Yes, a brain surgeon! A young, black female brain surgeon at that. I was in a room full of psychologists, therapists, surgeons, counselors, and even celebrities. At first, I felt out of place, because of my lack of credentials. However, I knew that I had something of value to offer my community, just like everyone else in attendance. So, I asked questions to everyone that would share their wisdom with me, and I vigorously took notes at every session.

Two sessions in particular struck a chord with me and prompted my mission to validate our black youth. The first session was called, *"Man Up: Real Talk about Men & Mental Health."* The presentation was curated by Dr. Michael Lindsey, who is the Director of the McSilver Institute for Poverty Policy and Research at NYU. Professor of Poverty Studies.

The first quote that Dr. Lindsey said was, "Love black men and children as if they've never been hated." I immediately realized exactly what our black boys needed, and that was love. This was something that I was qualified to offer, and I didn't need any degrees or certifications to do so.

My experiences and genuine heart to serve qualified me to identify, understand, and offer unconditional love. Not the watered-down version of love that is fabricated by material possessions or monotone expressions with no emotional backing. I would offer real love.

I later strategically broke down the word LOVE into an acronym which means to Listen, be Open-hearted, Validate, and Encourage. Offering this form of L.O.V.E. with an emphasis on validation was my offering to the next generation of young children of color.

Accompanied by my gift in writing literature, I created this book as a resource for you to empower and inspire young children of color across the country and even the world. The next session I attended was titled "*How are the children?*" During this session, I realized the real pain that children of color were facing daily.

"Students are coming to school with their backpacks but they are bringing more than just books with them," was a quote that was shared during the presentation. I started to think about my childhood and how true that statement was. "How could I help?"

I attended the conference to learn and apply to be of better service to my community. "What could I offer?" I was once told that "No one cares about your opinion." So, instead of offering my opinion on what I think can help our young Kings & Queens feel worthy, I decided to offer my gifts in writing and speaking as a source of light and inspiration for them.

With these letters of L.O.V.E., I hope to add resources within my mission to *CHANGE WHAT WE NORMALIZE™,* and eradicate the stigmas around mental health in children of color.

This book can be used as a daily resource to encourage and empower our children to excel in every area of their life. They will do so by knowing that they are descendants of royalty, that they are valued, and most importantly that they are loved. At this moment, I do not have a son, nor am I a father yet.

However, I've been a son and I'm a father-figure to many young black boys whose fathers are absent. Biologically, I am not a father, but I am a father in the sense of accepting the responsibility for helping raise and guide many young black boys into manhood successfully.

During my own experiences in helping to raise our young black boys, I've noticed that every child, especially our young black boys, without verbally saying it, wants our validation and guidance. You as an adult may even still want the validation of your Father.

The one question everyone on this planet shares no matter your race, creed, or age is, "Do I matter, and is my voice being heard?" This question is something that children ask themselves often. This question is one of the factors for a child's constant need for attention and also a factor in a lot of the misbehaviors of children.

With this book as a tool, we will not only validate our young black boys, but we will validate ourselves and work to increase our confidence.

"*Before we can pour into the cups of our children, we must first fill ourselves up.*"

My challenge to you reading is to be brutally honest with yourself. Ask yourself this question, "Who is my priority?" Statistically proven, the first person that people will claim as a priority are their children, a spouse, or another family member who is in their care.

While those answers are politically correct, the reality is that they are wrong. It's not that these important people in your life shouldn't be of a high priority to you, but if you aren't your priority then you do those people who you love a disservice. You can never give what you don't have. You must treat yourself as your priority.

If you aren't constantly striving to be the best version of yourself physically, mentally, emotionally, and financially then you are giving your loved ones a mediocre version of you. And if they are of high priority to you, then they deserve the best version of you that you can offer.

Anything else is unacceptable from this point moving forward. How will our boys continue to know their value once it's established? These questions are important because they will shape who our boys become and how they contribute to society.

What I will share next is how to apply real L.O.V.E. which consists of four steps that each child needs to experience to successfully feel valued from boyhood to manhood. To make this more practical, visualize a chair. Most chairs still utilize four legs to remain stable.

When one of those legs is not secure or missing, that chair becomes unstable and unsafe. Each leg of that chair is required for proper stabilization. Our boys are very similar in regards to their mental and emotional stabilization. When just one of these steps of L.O.V.E is inconsistent or missing, the risks of your boys becoming a statistic can increase.

Now, these four steps are not a quick fix, but with consistency and effort, they are extremely effective.

How should we
L.O.V.E. our black boys?

Step 1. Listen

Step 2. Open-heart

Step 3. Validate

Step 4. Encourage

Listen

A skillset that many people lack in today's society is this. It is a skill set that needs constant monitoring. Just like someone who wants to play basketball at a high level by practicing their game daily, we must practice listening daily. Ask yourself this question, "Am I able to listen to someone without interrupting them or tuning them out?"

This skill of listening alone will create a sense of self-worth in our boys. In a world where black boys are hyper-surveyed just in case, they do something wrong, where they are fighting to have their voices be heard, your undivided attention to their thoughts, ideas, and issues can increase their feeling of self-worth and ultimately build their self-esteem.

When someone attentively listens to you, a feeling of importance permeates your body and can shift the energy that you feel towards whoever is listening. It makes you want to share more with them because your bridge of trust has been built. Remember, the moment you stop listening is the moment you start ignoring.

Open-heart

Someone with an open-heart is someone that is not afraid to love. It is someone kind, compassionate, understanding, and honest. To have an open-heart means to have a willingness to feel and embrace emotions from others. This is crucial when approaching our black boys as their emotional response to you can be very strong. What looks like rage or disrespect at times, can be fear and insecurity.

An open-hearted approach allows them to see that your guard is down and it encourages them to lower theirs. Within this, a feeling will emerge that they can trust you, and it opens an opportunity to let go of past hurts by replacing it with new relationship opportunities. With an open-heart, there is an acceptance that is not based on conditions. Your open-heart approach should not be dependent on how they approach you or what they do for you.

Validation

Validation may be the most important step out of the four in regards to how we love our boys. Validation as defined by Dictionary.com is "The recognition or affirmation that a person or their feelings or opinions are valid or worthwhile." To validate someone is to be in acceptance of their feelings and emotions.

That is the beginning phase. When we validate our boys, we not only accept their experiences, we accept their thoughts, and also honor their experiences. This component is crucial because it will determine if they feel they are heard or not.

Validation requires you to acknowledge them which far too often does not happen, instead, they are often ignored. A lack of validation or approval, especially from men of the same cultural background, can devastate their self-esteem and beliefs about their self-efficacy as they mature in age. This makes validation a requirement if we ever expect to truly love and impact our black boys in a positive way that sets them up for success.

Encourage

What behavior have you encouraged through your actions? Has your behavior encouraged our boys to practice positive behaviors or discouraged them? How are you supporting our boys? All of these questions are important as they influence the actions that our boys take daily.

A black boy that is given support as well as hope, behaves differently than one who is ignored and discouraged. Now, to encourage someone else, you must first exude courage and confidence within yourself. This may require you to do some inner work before aiming to encourage someone else. Remember, your behaviors can encourage or discourage those around you.

Four action steps to help build self-esteem and self-efficacy in black boys

Step 1.
Appraisal - to set a value on; to evaluate the worth

Anyone who doesn't feel a sense of value, including your children, will feel worthless. When a child is born, the responsibility to add value to the child is that of the parents or guardian. Value goes as deep as what we name our children. Names, just like everything else in this world, have a meaning and a purpose.

This may seem insignificant but what you name your child is a reflection of who they are. Now, if you're reading this you have already named your child and that's fine. Nicknames are just as powerful as their government name.

Remember, when you call your child's name there is meaning behind that. For example, my parents named me, Nathan, which means (God's Child). Now I am a Jr., being that my Dad is Nathan Evans Sr. Whenever my parents call my name, there is power in knowing that my name has meaning, and I am God's child.

Again, this may not seem like a big deal to many parents, but I promise you there is power in what you name your child and what you say out of your mouth. To further evaluate your child's worth, you must wholeheartedly want your child to be better, do better, and contribute more to the world than you have.

This doesn't mean that you shouldn't strive for more or look at yourself as less than but to be fruitful and have dominion you must water your seed to blossom in ways that you could not. Your children are a direct extension of you and your greatness or lack thereof. An appraisal is the beginning step in validating your child and it starts with you, the parent.

Step 2.

Responsibility - liable to be called to account as the primary agent; accountability

A recurring issue that I find with a lot of troubled or rebellious children is a lack of responsibility. Responsibility can yield a feeling of worthiness and also accountability. Children are more likely to take pride in what they are being instructed to do if they have some form of ownership granted by their parents, teachers, and elders.

Barking orders has and will never make children or anyone for that matter feel worthy and/or important. That style of parenting has slavery traits within it. Your child is not your servant and they should not be treated as such. However, they should be appointed responsibilities in which they are to honor and occasionally be rewarded for when executed upon with a good attitude.

Step 3

Appreciation - a feeling or expression of admiration, approval, or gratitude

Appreciation and worthiness go hand in hand. You cannot have one without the other. Spontaneous celebratory actions are a simple yet effective way to display to your child the appreciation that you have for them. Now, these actions should be warranted to behavior that is deserving of such from your child. You should not be rewarding disrespect or laziness.

Once you open that can of tolerance for that type of behavior, it can become almost impossible to close. These types of behaviors must be addressed and adjusted. I remember for my thirtieth birthday, my dad surprised me with a party. He had my closest friends there, my fiancée and my family.

Even at the mature age of thirty years old, I still felt the overwhelming love and appreciation from my dad similar to when I was a seven-year-old kid. When I was seven years old, he would wake me up early on the weekends to randomly take me to the arcade, followed by pizza. Even as adults, your child will always have that feeling of worthiness whenever you display your appreciation for them.

The great thing about it was that he just wanted to hang out with me and let me know how much he loved and appreciated me. Too often do I hear parents say that their children don't appreciate anything but many of them haven't displayed their appreciation for their child. If that was you, it stops now. Changing what we normalize will impact generations upon generations, but it starts with you and it starts NOW!

Step 4
Purposeful Work - meaningful and intentional work to reach a dream

Parents and guardians, this last and final step of the "V4" concept are where your son will be able to display all of the value in which you have instilled in them. Purposeful work is usually attached to the moral code of a person. Purposeful work in which your child will perform will most likely happen within their late teen, young adult years.

None of these four steps in "V4" are meant to be a guaranteed plan to ensure your child lives a perfect life, but they are meant to be used as a guideline to ensure that your child is aware of the unconditional love that you have for them.

In *"The 5 Love Languages of Children: The Secret to Loving Children Effectively"* by Gary Chapman, he says that "Unconditional love will never spoil a child because it is impossible for parents to give too much of it." Conditional love is predicated off of what you can gain and not what you can give.

Table of Contents

Included at the end of this book are resources in the appendix including black psychiatrists, suicide statistics, training, books on behavioral health, and booking services provided by the author.

"Love black men and boys as if they've never been hated."

The Way of LOVE

[4] Love is patient, love is kind, it isn't jealous, it doesn't brag, it isn't arrogant, [5] it isn't rude, it doesn't seek its own advantage, it isn't irritable, it doesn't keep a record of complaints, [6] it isn't happy with injustice, but it is happy with the truth. [7] Love puts up with all things, trusts in all things, hopes for all things, endures all things. [8] Love never fails.

~ 1 Corinthians 13: 4-8

"We will place a crown over your head, but we won't place it on your head because you must grow to reach it."

Letters of LOVE from

NATE EVANS JR.

Young King,

I want to share with you some affirmations that come to mind when I think of you. These are affirmations that I would have taught my younger self to say but instead, I'll give them to you. I want you to read these aloud with confidence because they are true.

"This black boy is handsome."
"This black boy is intelligent."
"This black boy is creative."
"This black boy is valuable."
"This black boy is brave."
"This black boy is a scholar."
"This black boy is an owner."
"This black boy is a king."
"This black boy loves his community."
"This black boy is wealthy."
"This black boy can do anything."
"This black boy has no limits."
"This black boy is a child of God."
"This black boy is loved."

You are all these amazing things and so much more. I just wanted to remind you that you are great, you don't have any limits to what you can become, and you are loved!

I Love You,

~ Nate

Young King,

I remember feeling alone as I grew into a teenager and then into an adult. It was as if no one was experiencing the mental trauma that I was going through. I felt as if no one truly loved me and if I can be honest, I even discounted my parents' love because it was something I felt like they were obligated to do.

As time went on and I became older, I rebelled and searched for love in all the wrong places. I looked for love in women, partying, alcohol, money, and quick thrills. Nothing would fill this void. I felt even more empty while doing these things. It wasn't until I mended my relationship with God, that I started to feel at peace.

I grew up in the church. My mom and my great-grandmother never missed a service, prayer meeting, or revival. The issue was that I tried to borrow their faith and as a teenager and adult, but the reality was that I needed my own. Eventually, I would establish my faith and when I did, that love void was filled immediately and has never been empty since.

It's your responsibility to build your relationship with God as well. In this book, there will be multiple incredible black men that will share how much they love you, which is amazing. However, none of us can compare to God's love for you. Seek love there first and all the other love you'll receive will be a bonus!

I Love You,

~ Nate

Young King,

I won't demand you to "man up" or "grow up" as I do not want to take away from your childhood, with societal expectations but I will ask you to be responsible for your actions. As a Young King, you have the power to control your actions, your words, and as you will learn in this book, your thoughts.

Love and your mentality are your superpowers. Your mind is something that no one can take away from you and you have the power to strengthen it by learning daily and applying what you learn. Remember I always have and always will love you!

I love you,

~ Nate

Young King,

First, let me start by expressing how much I love you! I see myself in you daily. I look at you sometimes and just smile because your potential and optimistic energy just radiates from you. You have no boundaries to what you can accomplish, NEVER forget that.

It may seem like at times that the world is against you but that's not true. More people love you than you can ever imagine, and I'm included in that group. I want to prove to you through my actions just how much I love you every day. I won't be perfect, but I will always try my best to be a great example of what it means to be a man for you.

I love you,

~ Nate

Young King,

As I reflect on my life, I realize that I've made so many mistakes as a kid, teen, and even an adult now. What I've learned is that the key to progression is to not get down on yourself but to find out what the lesson is in the mistake. You will never be a failure if you continue to learn and progress.

Life unfolds into stages and in each stage, there are different seasons. In one season things may be going great for you! Everything you desire can be coming to fruition and life can seem perfect for a brief second. The next season you could suffer a great loss and face some traumatic experiences.

The thing is this, seasons don't last forever. One season you can feel like you are on top of the world, and in the next season, it can feel like your world is crumbling. Never get too low or too high on yourself. The goal is to have contentment knowing that the seasons will change. The key is also to prepare for the next season of your life.

As long as you are content in your mind knowing that life will have these highs and lows while also learning and applying what you learn every step of the way, you'll be fine, I promise. You got this, I believe in you!

I Love You,

~ Nate

"The moment you stop listening is the moment you start ignoring."

Letters of LOVE from

Ty Lewis

The Difference

Young King, did you know you were powerful? Did you know you possess a power that no one else in the world has? You are fearfully and wonderfully made. You were created with intention and purpose. In the center of your being, there is power. Your power is whatever sets you apart.

May I suggest that life itself is the journey to finding, understanding, and embracing the difference in you. This difference can take many forms. It could be physical, physiological, and emotional. It could come in the form of talent, syndrome, or disability. It could be a physical trait like a wide nose, red hair, or vitiligo.

Perhaps, your difference is your flamboyant personality or introverted seclusion. It could be that you were raised by your grandparents or a single parent. You may be the darkest shade of brown in your family or the lightest. Maybe you had to raise a sibling while your parents worked multiple occupations. You may have a way with words, or you shine as a leader.

Whatever your difference is that sets you apart, it is your power. That same power can open doors for you or close them. You have control of the narrative. Do not believe the lies of the enemy. You are powerful. If you are having difficulty comprehending this, you may need to change your perspective. I will explain it.

The enemy, society, the naysayers, the haters…they all say those powers I mentioned are inadequate. They all demean, belittle, judge, and antagonize you because of your difference. They would all rather you not celebrate your uniqueness, in their efforts to keep the light on them.

For one reason or another, you have fallen victim to the lies. I used to believe those tormenting lies as well. What I have learned is that the enemy's tactic is to deceive. If the enemy can grip your confidence, your destiny is sure to be suppressed.

Here is the good news, the Bible tells us that we were made in the image of God (Bible, Genesis 1:27.) If you were made in the image of a King; with intention and purpose, how could your design be powerless? You must fully understand who you are and from whom you were created.

When you enter a room, this understanding should enter with you with all authority and boldness. Your difference was given to you to cause conversation, open doors, change laws, speak up, bring awareness, change opinions, heal, deliver, and set free.

Your difference is not solely for you. It is also for all the lives that are called to you and your story. How more powerful could you be then to lead others to their destiny by embracing your image? There is nothing higher than this, I assure you. So, go forth Young King.

Regain your focus on the truth of God's word, shut the mouths of the naysayers, and live in your power. I expect nothing but greatness from you. Remember to be you out loud. Someone is looking for your light in a dark world.

"So God created human beings[a] in his own image.
In the image of God he created them;
male and female he created them." Genesis 1:27

I love you,
~Tyrell

Release

`

Young King, did you know that you don't have to be angry? Did you know that you don't have to keep your heart hardened forever? Did you know that you were allowed to smile? The weight you are carrying does not belong to you. You are not what happened to you.

You are not the choices someone made for your life, nor the consequences of those choices. You are not what they did to you. You are the wisdom, immunity, and life lessons that those experiences afforded you.

You may be walking around with misplaced anger. Mad at those who hurt you but directing that anger at your coach, teachers, mentors, and employers. While this is understandable; only you know the depth of your wounds, you could be potentially self-sabotaging your future.

You could be burning bridges to resources that you will need along your journey to success. You could be ruining relationships that were ordained to be your light along the path. I love you enough to tell you that you are worth more than the ashes of a failed future. You did not have control of the beginning of your story.

However, you can take back your life by simply surrendering the weight of hurt, rejection, and abuse. I know it seems impossible to imagine a life unchained to the worst parts of your life. When you have reconciled that you will only reach the level of success that the weight of anger will allow; it will seem impossible.

I too was so angry that I hated it. I hated all that had happened to me and those who caused my pain. Most of all, I hated how much power it had over me. Young King, I learned that I had to release myself from the weight of unforgiveness.

As soon as I identified who or what I was angry with, returned to them the responsibility of the offense and forgave them… I began to breathe again. My fists were no longer clutched, and my jaw loosened as I began to speak clearly and with certainty. No, forgiveness is not an overnight victory for anyone.

Yet, the process of forgiveness comes with a far lower cost than that of your destiny if you choose to ignore what you have learned. You have to allow yourself to become light. Choose yourself. Release everything that has happened to you or against you to God.

God says that He will perfect that which concerns you. If you can admit this weight is too heavy, He will bear it for you. Lift your hands where you are and surrender it all to God. Take a deep breath. You are doing it! I see your countenance rising already. I see your greatest self in the near future. I am so proud of you, Black King. You are winning. Freedom is yours.

"Love like you've never been hurt!"
~ Jentezen Franklin

I Love You
~ Tyrell

Accountability

Young King, STOP! If you are not willing to be held to a standard after you read this letter, stop reading now. This is not for the fragile. This is not for those who are on the path of excuses. This letter is intended for those who thrive from truth and correction. This letter is intended for those you seek wisdom and constructive criticism.

This is for those who want to stop using their disadvantages as a crutch. Yet, they would rather grasp the idea that their story is their foundation and an ordained necessity to their destiny. This letter is not for those cuddled or enabled to live beneath the call on their life. This letter is for those who want to be held accountable.

If you have read this far, I am to assume that you want to be on the front line of refinement and have accepted your right of passage into the Kingdom of Kings. Accountability is your portion.

Accountability can be defined as taking responsibility for your actions. Being accountable is a life of confession.

You will learn that the more you are willing to own, rather a bad decision, a lie, excuse, or an offense, the sooner you will accelerate to your destiny. How is this possible? Answer: The sooner you arrive at the truth; you have made a mistake, misjudged, were selfish or procrastinated, etc., the sooner you will learn the lesson that experience provided and you will then be granted access to the next level.

There is no need to be fearful of accountability. However, I encourage you to take a moment to exam yourself and to be honest. If you find the fear of responsibility, I assure you, you are not alone. Remember, you have read this far so you are ready to face that fear.

Identifying fear means you only need to change your perspective. Accountability is not a burden or a relinquishment of joy and reckless abandonment in your youth. Accountability is a badge of honor. It is a characteristic that makes the difference between a follower and a leader or borrower and a lender. It is a challenge and not to be taken lightly but it is a factor that will lead to your best days and greatest self.

When I look back, I wish someone was bold enough to love me so directly and firmly. I wish someone loved me enough to say, "You are wrong." I wish someone wouldn't have spared my feelings at the cost of my destiny at a much earlier age. I am humbled to inform you, who are reading this letter; I love you enough! I love you unconditionally. You are worthy of love.

Just like me, you may have been dealt a bad hand in life. You may have gotten a late start or need a second or even a fifth chance. Well, here it is my Young King. It's yours for the taking. Accept this challenge of holding yourself accountable in there will be no boundaries on where God can take you.

If you have read this far, you are now on the front line. I am so proud of you black King. Go forth boldly, standing in your rightful positions your ancestors died for. I'll be fighting on the front line with you. Let's win together!

I Love You,

~ Tyrell

The Chase

Young King, I can recall many times where I felt like I had gone too far. I felt like with each step I took off the beaten path the more unworthy I was of redemption. Discouraged, I continued down a narrow, dark road of anxiety and depression. Perhaps, you have been there, maybe you are there now.

In these moments, I wanted so desperately for someone to come and save me. I wanted someone to prove that I had not been forgotten. I wanted to feel that a second chance was possible. I could not always admit it but I knew I wanted to be loved and not alone.

A long journey someone brought to my attention a parable in the Bible. The parable was in the book of Matthew. I learned about a shepherd who left his flock of ninety-nine sheep to find the one that was lost. I was mesmerized at the thought of a love like this.

I could only wonder when my shepherd would come. This parable likened the shepherd to Jesus Christ. Once I welcomed the love of Christ into my heart; my eyes and heart were opened to so many shepherds who came to pour into my life. My shepherds came in the form of pastors, teachers, mentors, true friendships, and godly brothers.

They all stopped and came to my rescue, time, and time again. They left what was precious and valuable, just as the shepherd with the ninety-nine sheep, and made sure that I was counted. They loved me unconditionally, just because I was worthy.

Young King, this letter is me reaching out to you. Will you allow me to be a shepherd to you? I want you to know that I see you. I hear you. You and your hurt conditions matter to me. Just like the love of Jesus Christ, no sin could separate you from the love I have for you.

You are worthy of another chance. Grace and mercy are yours. Young King, love holds no record of wrong. Here is your fresh start. You are not alone. I am fighting for you. It's now time for you to take another shot at opening your heart and trusting. Trust that you are worthy of someone chasing after you and leading you to redemption.

You deserve all your heart's desires. Yet, are you willing to be led back to the light? I believe you are. Welcome back!

¹³ And if he finds it, I tell you the truth, he will rejoice over it more than over the ninety-nine that didn't wander away! ¹⁴ In the same way, it is not my heavenly Father's will that even one of these little ones should perish.

Matt: 18:13-14

I Love You,

Tyrell

"You can't give or receive love if your heart is closed."

Letters of LOVE from

TYWANE RUSSELL

Young King,

When you feel like no one cares about you, I LOVE YOU! We are one. I was you at one point in my life. This is why I've dedicated my adult life to let young men know what's possible for them. So many young men like yourself have taken the wrong path, looking for companionship, brotherhood, and love, not realizing they're searching in the wrong place.

My life's mission is to get you to understand you do not have to turn to the streets to receive love. Many brothers like myself have opened their hearts, minds, and arms to young men just like you. So don't be afraid to seek out these men and allow them to love you through mentorship.

Allow them to change your life for the better. We all need each other to survive and we all are connected. Therefore, never forget, you're always loved, Young King.

I love you,
~ Ty Russ

Young King,

When you feel like you don't have a voice, I hear you. I know, not too many people value the idea of listening, especially when you're young. You're speaking a different language through your actions and most people are only focused on their own life. I get it.

It's something you're going to have to get used to as well. You must learn how to withhold from exercising your voice to those who do not share your interest in the world. You must learn to use your voice for uplifting, healing, and positivity. When those messages become your normal language and actions, those who need to hear you will hear you. So never worry about "not being heard." I hear you, Young King. Keep speaking.

I love you,
~ Ty Russ

Young King,

When the world ignores you, I see you. I know it's tough out here, and I know how bad you want to be respected. I was the same way growing up, trust me. However, you must look to learn the difference between gaining respect and seeking attention. When you seek attention, you're chasing the wrong idea.

It's ok to be in the background doing your thing. That's the best way to gain respect. Pair "staying in the background" with "handling your business" and you can't go wrong. Not only will you gain attention, but you'll also gain the quality respect from those who know what's real out here.

Every day, I see young men like yourself, who have fallen victim to attention-seeking for fear of being ignored. And the same message I tell them is the same message I'm telling you, the people who matter the most are always watching. Those are the people you should want to make proud.

Those are the people that will be there when you fall. Those are the people that care enough to love you regardless of your flaws. So respect those people and pay those people with your actions and your love. And if all else fails, I'll be one of those people if you ever need me.

I love you,

~ Ty Russ

"Without a man's love & validation, our boys will seek for it in all the wrong places."

Letters of LOVE from

LES SQUAIR JR.

Real Big Things

*"When you have a growth mindset, the world becomes
your library and every day becomes a building block
to your success." ~ Les Squair Jr.*

Great Growthday Young Man,

*I want to be upfront with you, this series of letters are
extremely practical, meaning hands-on. You will be
motivated by each letter, but I want you to get more out of
this than just letters of encouragement and inspiration. I
want to empower you, so I am going to share some things
with you that I wish someone truly shared with me coming
up.*

*Then you can find a few execution steps after each letter
to make "Real Big Things" happen in your life. Are you
ready to make "Real Big Things" happen in your life?
Always do what will give you the advantage with integrity.
Integrity is doing the right thing when no one is watching.*

*The late great Kobe Bryant found what he wanted to
do in basketball at 13 years old and he used every resource,
every moment, every day to work on becoming the best. He*

was so focused in practice that you would think he was playing in a playoff game.

Kobe would practice by himself harder than others would work when their coach is watching. That type of effort will lead you to success. By working on himself, he advanced to a higher level than his competition. He worked on him! I'm not saying that you need to know exactly what you want right now, but work on "you."

In the execution steps below, I don't want you to just try these steps. I would love for you to practice them every day. Here is how you work on you.

Execution Steps:

1.) Read one letter in this book every day.

2.) Take a picture of the letter you read, post it with something you learned, and tag all your friends.

I Love You,

~ Les

Grow Through It

"The better you become, the more you are able to do."
~ Les Squair Jr.

Great Growthday Young Man,

If no one has shared this with you before, allow me to walk you through this. The pain of losing something or someone that you care about so much is tough. Growing up with unfortunate circumstances seems unfair. Experiencing your first heartbreak hurts.

Coming up short, failing a test, or falling flat on your face is annoying and embarrassing. Yes, I know, but it is those moments that help you build exceptional character. Plus, the trouble/pain won't last always, the challenges are temporary. Joy will come in the morning.

You know what, let me just break it down for you like this; have you ever watched an action movie that didn't have any adversity in it? Most likely you haven't because what sells the movie is a great story. Great stories include the challenges that the characters experience.

We want to know how they break free, how'd they destroy their enemy, or how the characters just rose above the madness. This is what makes a great story. My point is, you have to grow through those moments because you'll get better. The better you become the more you can do. The more that you are capable of overcoming, the greater your story/movie. Think about some of the great things that you want to do.

Pain should never be wasted. If you are going through something, you should find the lesson in what you have experienced. This will decrease fear, increase your faith, and give you a level of peace that brings you confidence in challenges and tests. Ultimately, your pain and challenges bring purpose, so embrace them, you will progress through life with less stress

Execution Steps:

1. *) Write down three great goals you want to accomplish.*
2. *) Then write down three steps that can help you get closer to each great goal.*
3. *) Read your great goals and steps each day.*

I Love You,

~ Les

Legacy over Everything but God

"Learning is the foundation of living a great life."

~ Les Squair Jr.

Great Growthday Young Man,

Let me start by saying, I LOVE YOU! *There is a level of fulfillment that every young man needs. We all go through phases and each phase we need to be validated with an order of encouraging words like, "You got what it takes, you are enough, I am very proud of you, and I love you." In the same breath, we need a patient guide, our father to be exact, to take the time to instruct, acknowledge, and correct us. But when we aren't validated in this way, no father present, we go seeking validation. Sometimes people seek validation in very dangerous or in poor environments like gangs, drugs, and alcohol abuse, abusive relationships, etc. and sometimes we even seek validation through what the world solely portrays as successful such as; football, basketball, entertainment, money, women, titles, etc.*

There is nothing wrong with pursuing success, just make sure that you don't exalt success as your source of peace. Peace comes from one place, that place is in God. The

41

validation that we seek is ultimately in God our heavenly father, and our earthly father is supposed to make that introduction and be in alignment with God so that he can teach us how to seek wisdom, to have faith, believe in Jesus Christ, be aligned with God's will, so forth and so on. When we are missing our earthly father in our lives, there is a strong void that we try to fill. Unfortunately, we then try to find God in everything else. That is why when most young men build a real relationship with God, He fills that void of their earthly fathers' absence.

No real man can be successful without God, he will always fall short because we are flawed and born into sin. Sin and flaws of our flesh will always solely chase after what the world views as success. But when we are in alignment with God, He orders our path and we experience peace. Worldly success and heavenly peace are completely different. In everything that you do, seek the truth.

Oh yeah! And last but certainly not least, develop a growth mindset. Meaning, keep an open mind to learning all that you can never settle. Learning is the foundation of living a great life. Dedicate your life to become better every day, in every area of your life. Remain a great student, keep learning, and never become complacent. I use this term, Go for the gusto! Which means, everything that is available to you, go get it. You were born for greatness, but the world sometimes conditions us to be average and mediocre. But that's not you, that's not your problem. You were born with gifts and talents. You must discover your gifts and use them for good.

Legacy has everything to do with your purpose in life. What you do here on earth with your time will either be forgotten or always be remembered. The people that are always remembered and create a legacy are the people that build something beyond themselves. They disrupt the status quo and push barriers. They make things better. The world is better because of them.

Execution Steps:

1.) *Go to one of your local banks and start a savings account.*
2.) *Learn the basics of taxes.*
3.) *Learn the difference between profits and wages.*

I love you,
~ Les Squair Jr.

Stewardship over Ownership

"The impact of ownership may spread in your lifetime, but Great Stewardship leaves an effective impact in many ways that lasts forever." ~ Les Squair Jr.

Great Growthday Young Man,

I would be doing you a disservice if I didn't share this next thought; which is, never jeopardize your freedom, your life or tarnish your reputation and influence by making decisions that are forever. What I mean is, you are too valuable to be locked behind bars, dead, or viewed as broken, busted, and/ or disgusted. So stay out of trouble and when trouble finds you, get out of there immediately with reason. You have a purpose for your life, you don't need to be limited by foolish decisions by you or anyone else. You need to have access to every opportunity that is available to you.

I know that may seem like a lot of pressure but it's just choices. The better choices you make the better your life will be. Some people choose to stay in survival mode and others choose to live. What will be your choice?

I should remind you that; You are a King! You are Supreme! You have dominion here on earth! You already have the victory! Where I'm from, we call "victory" a "dub" short for "W" or in other words, "the win."

You must live your life with the mindset that you already have the dub, not to be arrogant but to operate with confidence and humility. You are occupying this position as a King for the time you are here, make the best of it. Remember a King's reign is temporary but passed on to the next generation. So here's the game! The secret sauce! Are you ready?

Here's how you make the best out of your role as a King; become a great steward. I know you are probably like, what are you talking about, but hear me out first, then make an informed decision. Being a great steward means that you are a careful and responsible manager of something entrusted to your care. You are entrusted with your life. You are entrusted with anything you acquire in your lifetime.

That goes for relationships, money, real estate, influence, your talents and gifts, your family, etc. We cannot take anything with us when we leave this place but we can take care of it and elevate whatever was given to us while we are here. The mindset of ownership is a trick because ownership breeds selfishness and possessing things that are never really yours. It's a nonstop pursuit of unhappiness, you are unable to have peace and joy with ownership.

The reason why is because if it can be taken away from you then it isn't yours. That's the trick! So the world will have you stressed out pursuing success based on what you own and the titles you acquire, whereas being a great steward is a peaceful and joyful process of growing what God has provided. Don't believe me, try not paying for your cell phone bill, the company will turn it off. Try not going to work, you won't get paid and the chances of you getting fired are high. But as a great steward, the mindset is, I don't feel the pressure of possessions, titles, etc. I feel peace and joy while I carefully and responsibly manage what I am given.

Now, the reason you manage these things carefully is that you must leave an inheritance for your children's children, relationships, financial freedom, assets, real estate, family history, family documents, education, etc. So, anything that you acquire over your lifetime, you ought to manage it with great care because someone else will occupy that position that you are in one day. You can position your family's peace, joy, and future with the efforts of a great steward. The purpose of us being here on earth is to make it better, so if you are a great steward, then your living isn't in vain.

So after all of that, I have to ask this question; are you going to get out of this life alive? That's a rhetorical question, the answer is of course not! As we all will pass away at some point, and we cannot take everything that we work so hard to get and to own with us, what's the point of ownership? The greatest thing we can do is to go as hard as we can to build up our family and as many people as we possibly can. Don't make decisions based on ownership, make decisions based on Great Stewardship.

"The impact of ownership may spread in your lifetime, but Great Stewardship leaves an effective impact in many ways that lasts forever."

Execution Steps:

1.) *Write down all the things that you possess.*
2.) *Next to what you possess, write down if you are being a great steward or not.*

3.) *All that you possess that you aren't being a great steward over, start.*

I love you,

~ Les Squair Jr.

"Where there is hope, there is an opportunity for progression."

Letters of LOVE from

MICHAEL FOREST

Be grateful

Peace King,

One thing I've learned over the years is to understand that the best of things may not happen today. Daily, as men, we picture our days to go exactly how we may have envisioned it. We wake up, eat breakfast, and go about our day without a thought of things possibly going wrong. I believe when we understand that at any moment things could take a turn for the worse, we prepare ourselves spiritually and mentally to embrace those moments. You may be angry about some things, you may be holding some things inside, and with those feelings plus any unexpected moment could lead to a disaster.

King, I'm writing you this letter so that you may be prepared, that you may overcome any obstacle that may come to break you today or ANY day in your future. Stay prayed up and strong spiritually these days. Don't expect your days to be horrible, but don't expect them to be perfect either. Allow yourself to understand things will come and you are prepared to win! We can control only ourselves and the reactions we may display.

Today, choose to be positive no matter what the world throws at you. Embrace every moment, good and the bad, and grow in your manhood accordingly. Remember to never give anything or anyone power over you and your reactions. Win today and every day after!

I Love You,

~ Michael

A fatherless son is what you might be but who's to say a father is what you can't be?

Peace King,

A fatherless son is what you might be but who's to say a father is what you can't be? Since I was a child, I had the desire to be a father and not only a father but a husband as well. Growing up in a single-family home had its hard times as a young man. I remember living in an area where most of my good friends had their father in the house with them. When we played football with each other those same fathers would sometimes play "steady QB" and make that experience of playing football so much fun.

My friends always had that look like they wished their father would leave or stop playing with us, but I was thinking how cool it was for them to be around. I used to say to myself, "One day this will be me playing with my sons and their friends." Some young men use the absence of their father to fuel anger and tend to act out of character at times. If that is you, trust me I understand, but I chose to use that same anger as motivation to be better. I remember the way I felt as a child, being alone, wishing to have those talks about girls and sports but never had the opportunity to do so.

Those thoughts lead me to make some of the best decisions in my life. While most of my friends were having sexual encounters with multiple females just because they could, I was focusing on making sure the women I was with I could see as the mother of my child and a possible wife. This lifestyle I chose kept me out of a lot of trouble and helped me to grow in my fatherhood one day. I grew up with my brother and sister in a two-bedroom home along with my mother. My siblings and I all had different fathers and would some days be split up during the summers and weekends.

We hated being separated and that feeling is something I always remembered. When I was ready, I wanted to be a husband to a wife and start a family where our kids would never be separated. When I tell you I was having these aspirations at the age of eight years old you would think I was tripping at such a young age.

I see those times as God speaking to me about how important Fatherhood meant to me and I knew for sure there were other young men like me having these same dreams, maybe even you reading this passage right now. I was a fatherless son and maybe you are too, but who's to say a father is what YOU can't be?

A son needs his father and a father needs his sons. Continue to think about your future sons and how you will be the greatest father they could ever imagine. You will be an amazing husband and father when the time is right! I pray that you save this passage and revisit it from time to time as motivation to continue to dream of one day being the best you possible so that your future son can NEVER be fatherless.

I Love You,
~ Mike

Success is personal

Peace King,

The word "success" gets thrown around a lot in today's society. I'm sure you have heard it quite a bit while you're figuring out your life journey. With social media in our faces every day, it's so easy to measure yourself up with others. When looking at your social media accounts, or maybe checking out a show on television, many visions are portrayed and fed to the minds of our younger generation.

It's so easy to measure your success to others and when it doesn't measure up to what you see, you don't "feel" successful. With people holding money to their ear on almost every post or seeing a man with a beautiful woman on his hip in these news feeds, it's VERY easy to get discouraged because you never seem to have the same "success."

Young King, understand that success is personal! Success can only be measured by your heart and passion. It's easy to feel unsuccessful in trying to have someone else's success. You don't feel as if you're living YOUR dream because that success is not YOURS.

Ask yourself: what is successful to me? What are some things you would consider successful? When I was a young man, all I wanted was to be married with kids and be a Father to my sons. I accomplished that so in my mind I'm successful and no one can tell me otherwise.

When you have personal success guidelines, your chances of comparing yourself to others or feeling discouraged can be eliminated because it's a personal task for yourself. Growing up I always wondered why horses had those blinders on their eyes when they walked the streets pulling the carriages.

When I learned it was for focus and them to remain on the path and not get sidetracked, I understood. It's so easy to look to the side or behind and see what's going on and lose focus. Young King, I would encourage you to put the blinders on and remain focused on your success path. Be great, be comfortable, and most importantly, BE YOU!

I Love You,
Mike

Respect should be given, even if it's not earned.

Peace King,

The world we live in today is a scary one. Many of our young kings end up in some serious situations that most often lead to trouble or even death. My mother used to always tell me growing up that there will be people out to get you regardless of how good a person you are. My mother would say, "Kill people with kindness, it hurts them more when you show love and respect."

I feel that line from my mother has so much meaning in today's society. I understand that every person we come in contact with will not deserve our respect. Some people are just plain horrible and live to see the downfall of others, but respect should be given even if it's not earned.

There was a time when I worked in a school system where teachers would try to push the buttons of some of the students I had in my anger management sessions. Mind you, most of these students didn't have anger issues but that's another story. I would tell them to respond positively at all costs. I would tell them to try it even when it hurts to the core. *The goal was to remain respectful and report back to me if anything escalated.*

Almost every interaction where I told the student to be respectful there were no signs of escalation. One of my students told me that a teacher apologized for being negative towards him. In most instances in life, we have to understand the importance of respecting authority. I will tell you now that every authority figure will not deserve your respect, but it must be given.

Most young people walk around with the "if you want respect you gotta earn it" mantra and trust me I understand the motive but most times that doesn't lead to desirable outcomes. Authority figures know when they are being disrespectful and often think back on situations where they may have stepped out of line.

At times, the authority figure may not know how to apologize but will often do something "kind" to show how they may have done wrong. Often that feeling of remorse is short-lived because the response from the young man can lead to words and actions that can't be taken back, and in most cases lead to suspensions, fights, or even jail time.

It's in those times I hope that the person reading this passage can take a lesson from my mother I learned years ago, and that is to remember to kill people with kindness and keep all of your power within and use it positively. The moment you give your power to someone else is the moment you lose control of the situation.

Next time a situation arises, and you feel that this person does not deserve your respect, remember to kill them with kindness.

I Love You,

~ Mike

Our women deserve the best.

Peace King,

It's time to stand up and be better men for our women! During my thirty-nine years of life, I have seen a lot when it comes to our queens. I've had friends who treated young ladies like property and had no care in the world for them. I was once caught up with thinking the more women I had the cooler I was.

I soon found that was a lie and I also found out it was hard work trying to please more than one young lady. During that whole process, hearts were broken and relationships that were thought to be solid would be diminished. I'm not saying that every young lady you meet is the one you should try to settle down with, I'm saying let's have some respect for our women and be builders not breakers.

Many of our young ladies feel they have to dress a certain way or act a certain way to attract a young man. It's up to us to let them know that it's the best situation only when each young lady is comfortable in their skin. The world needs the best each young lady can provide.

A young King's voice means so much in the community today. We need to speak up and tell our friends, family, and female friends the truth with love. My only hope is for whoever is reading this passage, will one day have the wife of your dreams. I hope and pray that you speak to God about the type of woman you see yourself with.

Tell God everything you desire in a wife and watch Him provide as you respect and honor our young Queens in the meantime. I shared in this book in another passage how growing up I would not have relations with anyone I couldn't see myself having a kid with or marrying in the future.

Things happen, unexpected pregnancies and bad choices could happen to anyone. I made sure that if any unexpected child was to ever happen in my life, it would be with someone that I would give my last name to and become a husband and a father. I know this is a hard path to choose to walk but I'm sharing this because you are no different than me.

We all have the willpower to make choices and I believe that you will make the best choices of your life starting today! I see you as a great man, father, and husband in the future.

I see you treating our young queens with love and respect even if they are not your significant other.

You're doing it because it's the right thing to do and God is watching your movement and counting you worthy of the women He will send to you to help you become the greatest man you can be. The day I met my wife in college is the day when I changed forever. My wife makes me better, she supports and loves me unconditionally, and she gave me two amazing sons that I live for! I can't wait to read your story one day! Peace King, Peace.

I Love You,

~ Mike

"I see you and I hear you.
I can't ignore your greatness."

Letters of LOVE from

ALEX SPEAKS

Young King,

I have so much respect and love for you. I see you as a Sir. Let me explain to you why in my letters that I wrote to you.

Hello Sir

Hello Sir!

The reason why I called you Sir is because it's defined as a respectful way of addressing a man. I know you are not currently a man right now, but becoming a man is a choice. Trust me there are many grown males out there that are still acting like they are your age. Would you like to know how to become a man? I'm glad you asked! You see, a man is one who takes responsibility instead of pointing the finger at everyone except himself.

When I say "take responsibility", meaning take advantage of the opportunities afforded to you, maximize the relationships you have, exercise discipline in refraining from your vices, and last but not least trust that God will always make a way out of no way. You were born to be a man, to give respect, and you were born to be mad; which means Make A Difference! Never forget that being a man has ALL to do with serving others more than serving yourself. Congratulations Sir, you've just been promoted.

I Love You,

~ Alex

Hello Sir!

I want you to think big but I don't want you to think big in the form of a fantasy. You see, fantasy is the imagery of things hoped for without you putting the work in. In this life, you will have to go through many trials to obtain what is rightfully yours. Thinking big is seeing yourself as a hard worker, faithful to one wife, dedicated to the function of fatherhood and submission to authority.

Thinking big has nothing to do with living your best life; thinking big has all to do with you laying down your life for a higher purpose. I need you to understand that you can only go as far as your thoughts. Don't let fear keep you from pursuing what your parents never achieved and don't let people talk you out of ignoring that burning desire that is cooking on the inside of you.

Please do not fall into the trap of fantasizing about unrealistic things and meditating on possible future mishaps because that is what small thinkers do. Think big and shoot for the moon because even if you miss, you will land among the stars.

I Love You,

~ Alex

Hello Sir,

I want you to know that you are your brother's keeper. I know you are saying, "I am too young to be responsible for anyone." Sorry, you are! You are more influential than you can ever imagine. Everyone is watching you and there are things about you that are helping people and are probably hurting people. When you become older, you'll be surprised by the certain negative behaviors you may exhibit that you got from someone years ago.

Somebody is watching how you treat girls, watching how you respect your parents, watching you as a student, and watching to see if you are a trouble maker or peacemaker. So, what are you doing? Are you trying to be cool to win the approval of others? Because if you are, several years down the line you will admit how foolish that was.

My advice to you is to be you. Look in your mirror more than looking at someone else. Everybody is watching, but let them see you becoming the best version of you and that is how you will be a great brother's keeper.

I Love You

~ Alex

Hello Sir,

I just want you to know that when I think of you; I think of a Prince. A Prince is defined as the son of a King. He inherits all of what his daddy left him without doing all of what his daddy did. Keep in mind; I'm not talking about your natural daddy, I am talking about your Heavenly Father also known as God. There is no way you can function as a prince here on earth without being in a relationship with your Heavenly Father. He is your creator and if you ever want to know your purpose, never ask yourself that question, only ask the Creator.

You were created by God, in the image of God, so do me a favor and NEVER try to be or act like anyone! Your presence is not a mistake, but intentional. You are unique and custom made for a specific cause. How you discover that cause is praying often, reading your Bible daily, serving others, and exercising discipline in all temptations. You are a Prince that is connected to a Royal Priesthood so on no account; do not ever believe that you are alone.

I Love You

~ Alex

Hello Sir,

In the previous letter, I wanted to strongly emphasize that you are a Prince, but now I want to let you know what your future looks like. Your upcoming adult life will be nothing short of a King. Princes are raised by Kings to become Kings themselves. That's why you should always address your girlfriend like a princess and when she becomes your wife you will acknowledge her as your Queen.

Listen here future King, you are to ALWAYS treat every female with respect, honor, and never physically abuse them. Females are God's gift to a man that should be treated as an equal partner and not as one who is below you.

Jesus is known as the King of kings which means you are the lowercase "k." Please, future king, submit to the Lord in all HIS ways on how to treat your grandmother, mother, aunt, sister, and any female you encounter. Don't do it for me, do it for HIM because HE needs your help in using you as HIS partner in developing more princesses and queens here on the earth. I am thanking you in advance because your future is a very bright, good job King!

I Love You

~ Alex

"*You matter, and so does your future.*"

Letters of LOVE from

DARRELL EDMONDS

Young King,

I see you working hard, and I know it's not easy. Things didn't go according to your plan, but you are continuing to pursue your dreams. In some ways, that's an accomplishment in itself. . . to continue to work hard and persevere after a setback. I'm proud of you. I also know that I'm not the only voice.

Others are telling you that you can't do it. Saying that you might as well just join them on the corner or in the trap. But that's exactly what it is, a trap. You know there is more for you and that you have been created for great things. Don't ever lose sight of that. Those other voices may be louder at times, but nothing is greater than your purpose. Hold on tight to your dreams and keep moving forward

I Love You,

~ Darrell

Young King,

I heard you loud and clear when you said that people only see you when you have football pads on. How you have been made to feel that your value is greater as a football player than as a student or a person. You have amazing self-awareness at your age to be able to identify and articulate those feelings. I'm proud of you. That "thing" that you feel, that lets you know that you are more than just a football player, is golden.

Hold on to it as tight as possible. On the flip side, I'm sure you enjoy the sport. Perhaps you even love it. I've been there myself. Not only did I love the sport, but I loved the daily affirmation that I got from achieving on the field. But there's always that "thing" that lingers. That part of you that says, "If you think I'm good at football, just wait until you get to really know me." Let them know who you are!

I Love You,

~ Darrell

Young King,

If you haven't heard it lately, let me tell you that I love you. I know you are going through something incredibly difficult right now. It causes you to ask the question, "Why me?" I really can't speak to why, but I can speak on YOU. You are one of the most gifted young men I know. This difficult time hasn't defined you, but it has refined you and I'm proud of you.

Honestly, you are one of the most gifted young men I've ever met. You are bright, musically gifted and you see things from a different perspective. Your unique perspective is a gift. You don't just look at the bright side, you see four to five different sides to a situation and you figure out a way to excel in any situation. Keep excelling and carving your path. What you are dealing with, is not your ending but only a redirection toward your true purpose.

I Love You,
~ Darrell

"Black boys are smart. Black boys are great. Black boys are loved."

Letters of Love from

RICARDO BELGRAVE

I am your responsibility.

Young King,

I hope this letter finds you well. I know things have been difficult during this transition in your life, however, I am here to let you know...YOU ARE MY RESPONSIBILITY. I say this with a heart full of love, passion, and purpose. I say this knowing full and well that we are not connected through blood, but we are connected through kinship and in spirit. I say this because I am charged with a divine command to take on the responsibility of speaking life into your existence. Speaking truth to power and speaking positivity into your universe.

Always remember that when things get tough, YOU ARE MY RESPONSIBILITY. And as a man, I do not take that lightly. Because when a man has a responsibility, he must adhere to the task necessary to ensure that responsibility is taken care of. Anything less is unacceptable! So, always remember Young King, you are not alone and as a responsible man, you can always count on me.

I Love You,
~ Ricardo

Wins and Losses

Young King,

I wanted to let you know about a little thing I call the "wins and losses" concept. So many people get caught up in whether they are winning the "game of life" or not. However, I want to share with you the fact that Life is a continued effort of becoming the best version of yourself as possible and a part of that process is understanding that you are going to take some "L's" along the way. Think of it like this...The NBA has 82 games in a total season. NO TEAM has ever gone 82 and 0.

NEVER...Even two of the greatest teams in NBA history lost 9 and 10 phenomenal games! What does that mean? It means everyone is entitled to lose and learn. Now, if you accumulate enough losses then you will find yourself "out of the playoffs" and not in a position to even compete in the "game of life"...i.e., jail or death.

Your goal every day should be to accumulate as many wins as possible to one day become a champion of your passion and Purpose in life. If you find yourself reflecting on your day and feeling like you caught an "L," that's cool, just learn the lesson necessary to move on and get a win the next day.

I Love You,

~ Ricardo

Breaking chains of oppression

Young King,

Generation after generation of Black men have been struggling to survive in a world designed to keep them down but I want you to know that your existence is special because you are equipped with the tools to break the chains of oppression. Always remember you are the BEST VERSION of your ancestors. They sacrificed and went through turmoil so you wouldn't have to. You may ask yourself, why? Well, it's because each previous generation has to do what is necessary to make things better for the one to come after.

Now it is your turn! And with the guidance of the Men in your life and the support of people who truly care about you, you will be the next one to break another chain of oppression. Stand up and take on this task Young King! It is a badge of honor. There is beauty in the struggle, take pride in it, and don't forget that someone did it for you and now you have to do it for someone coming after you.

I Love You,

~ Ricardo

"*I see you and I hear you;
I can't ignore your greatness.*"

Letters of LOVE from

Alan Laws Jr.

Young King,

You are now coming into that age when you begin to understand what's going on around you. You are beginning to know the difference between wants, needs, and that life will bring forth much of both. I want you to realize that those things you want will always be so attractive, loud, and shiny, but as you have heard, everything that glitters ain't gold. Those wants, not always, but in many cases will lead down many paths of confusion. These wants will come in the form of people, places, and things and they all will appear to accept you with open arms, but I tell you every open door is not the right option, every pretty smile is not the right person, and all the finer things won't make you happy. Now the needs, are the vital things in life, that make you who you are.

Young King, you are now at a time when you have to take a look at the man in the mirror and first, and ask yourself for as long as you need, then remind yourself every day after, who you are. Know that God has perfectly made you. Your path to greatness has been laid out for you, and life will be what you make it. As paved as this path is for you, it will still call for you to make the right decisions, being that life is a sum of all choices. I say to you now, don't choose with your eyes, don't choose with your ears, don't even choose with your touch, but choose with your heart and with your faith which knows your heart. And even now as a young man when it seems that outside of your parents, your girl, and your children, that Love doesn't exist, know that it is everlasting.

Love is true, love is hard, love is real. And when love still seems that it is not enough, let your love for God and God's love for you, be the compass that guides you through this life that is ahead. And after you take it all in, you teach that baby boy that you are raising what it feels like to be loved, what it looks like to show love, and what it is to know love.

I Love You

~ AJ

Young King,

I wanted to do something a little different for my last letter to you. I wrote a few poetry pieces for you instead of writing traditional letters. I hope that they reflect my love for you. Enjoy Young King, and I love You!

Letter to Baby Boy

Dear Baby Boy,

When you open your eyes and are finally able to see this world for what it is, I want you to know that it is yours for the taking. I don't want you to come into this world with the mindset that the odds are against you and that you are meant to fail. I want you to know that the burden will get heavy, and the walls will close in fast at times but all it takes is for you to reach.

Reach out your hand and say, "Lord I need your help and can't do this by myself." You do this and I can promise you that the days will get better, the weight will get lighter, and those doors of opportunity will open. It may not always be in your time, it will always be on time.

Baby Boy, in this world that you are coming into, there is a lot of hate and sometimes pure evil, but I want you to know that love conquers all things and before your life even began you were loved. Attract and attach yourself to all the love this world has to offer and allow it to overwhelm the hate. And when it feels like there is just not enough love, love God, love yourself, and know that you are loved by me.

I Love You

~AJ

The Remedy

Looking for a source or outlet to alleviate the pain, when in all reality these remedies will only deviate the pain. I rather go forth, address life, and mediate the pain. Meet it halfway to expedite the pain. Head on into a storm where I can't see the days end, my mind so clouded, wondering when the daze ends.

Stuck on yesterday for self-preservation, but this life needs no invite or a reservation. It's one that you've earned and yearned to live in, but now that the pain is a stain, you want to give in; to a temporary remedy and a fix that will fail, you feel you're in a prison of suffering, praying one day you post bail. To get out of this rain that's so heavily pouring, and subside the pain that you're so heavily gorged in.

But this whole time you've been thinking that pain is your enemy when what's built off of pain has always been the remedy. What has pain taught us, is to withstand and seek relief, but beneath all the hurt one has to seek belief. Belief in the fact that pain is inevitable, it comes and it goes with a cause immeasurable.

Still looking for a remedy for aches you can't heal, searching an enemy whose face you can't feel. Pain! It breaks us with its scars, pain! It makes us who we are. Pain! It teaches as it hurts. Pain! Value what it's worth.

Still hoping for a remedy that could take all the pain away, when growth is the remedy, built off of your pain today. So stop searching and hoping, giving pain your energy, because what pain has created has always been the remedy.

I Love You

~ AJ

"*What is invisible is often what is most valuable, and that includes LOVE.*"

Letters of LOVE from

Tiriq Callaway

Young King, I wrote a series of pieces for you titled, "An E-Pill a Day." We live in a time where so many of your peers are losing their lives to drugs because they are trying to escape their reality. I want to give you something that will bring life to you and not take it away. I love you too much to allow you to hurt yourself.

Embrace

As children and young adults, we were all told to learn from our mistakes. What wasn't explained to us, was to embrace the struggles that often arise, despite our faults. At times, we are overwhelmed with those life battles, and can't seem to find our way. The experiences become so mundane, that we cope by numbing ourselves from the pain. We rely on drugs, sports, music, and other mechanisms to mask the hurt that we feel inside.

The truth is, when the music stops, sports is over with, and sobriety kicks in, those same feelings we avoided for so long, come back to the surface. No matter how long we run from the trauma that exists, it still resides within. It's important to first acknowledge the conflict in our lives because when we are in denial, it stunts us from our full potential. This confession alone segues into many possibilities

*for our personal growth. The essential step toward evolution
is when we embrace all the turbulence in our lives.*

I Love You,

~ Tiriq

Emancipate

As a Black man, you may feel an obligation to have to look over your shoulder wherever you travel in the world. Whether it be you having to protect yourself from your race, or being extremely anxious about others, it could be quite debilitating. I know the feeling all too well, especially being a black man with dreads. You are perceived by how you dress, speak, and ultimately based on the color of your skin. You may feel like you're not free to be who you are because of stereotypical views.

Some of you even conform to society's pressure, and your light is dimmed due to the oppressor. It's time for you to move from the past, narrate your own story, and create a better future. It's simple to stick to the normality of how the world operates, but you are meant to be special.

Unique people stand out and make things happen for themselves and others. You have a gift inside of you that you may not even understand or even tapped in to yet. I'm here to inform you that you matter, regardless of how anyone views you. Bring your dreams to life and show yourself that your potential is limitless.

As soon as you free yourself from the locks that society has put on your mind, you'll reveal so many possibilities for you and your future – and soar to unimaginable heights.

I Love you,

~ Tiriq

Express

There has always been much made about how males don't show emotion in particular ways; specifically crying. Some moments in history told all of us men that shedding a tear was weak. Oddly enough, we walk around with the weight of the world on our shoulders, weakening our thoughts while making irrational decisions.

We act out without even thinking, putting ourselves in unfortunate predicaments that lead us to a path of darkness. It is self-destruction at its best, as our true feelings are suppressed. It's time to change this narrative.

We do ourselves a disservice when we don't release any tension or pain of the past. We carry a load of emotions and act out angrily. Whatever feelings you have about your dad not being there, your mom not being able to provide as much as you wanted, and ultimately you feeling trapped in a situation you think you can't escape from, CRY IT ALL OUT!

Cry, because it is your right to do so, and don't hold back because someone told you to "man up." It takes a lot of courage for a young man to cry based on what we've been taught not to do for centuries. Crying is one of the strongest expressions of our feelings. Whether it be due to sadness or happiness, cry with a purpose – realizing that all the burdens and agony are released through the tears that fall upon our face. Let the tears be the relief we need to be that much closer to self-gratitude.

I Love You,

~ Tiriq

Evolve

To get to the next step in our lives, we must be willing to do the work. We shy away from speaking to others about our situations when we really should be talking it out with someone. We blamed others instead of holding ourselves accountable. We join organizations for protection and acceptance, yet we are insecure with our reflection. We could run to whoever or where ever we find comfort, but it starts and ends with having a love for ourselves.

We must be comfortable with who we are as individuals, despite how others view us. How we are perceived, we have no control over, so we must focus on who matters most: YOU! The love we should have for ourselves has nothing to do with anyone else. Don't ever attempt to fit in, because when we do, we live and die by others' expectations of us.

Set goals for yourself and stick to them regardless of how tough life gets, go to any extent to ensure your progress, love life and the process of it, and evolve into the young man you're made to be. Life is that much grander when we grow through all the hardships we had to endure.

I Love You,

~ Tiriq

Embody

There is a subconscious connection to our ancestral roots. I can honestly say, when I was younger, I didn't necessarily care about these things. I was too self-centered and worried about my issues, and how someone can help my situation. This might be the same feeling in your life right now. You only care about how someone could help position you. The fact and the matter is, the fate of your future depends on YOU.

Our ancestors have everything to do with our existence though. Think about how they've fought for so much to be free – to give us a chance to be where we are right now. Furthermore, think about their fight alone with racism and for their human rights overall.

We are in a similar battle today – as we struggle with being seen and heard as African Americans period. As young black men, you have a voice, and it's important to use it for the greater good of your future, and generations after you.

I'm not saying take on the responsibility of leading everyone, but more so, be aware of the things you do and say. You are an example whether you want to be or not, because you are looked at – whether it be in a good or bad light.

Question is, are you going to set a great tone, or continue to be a part of the status quo? You are a natural-born leader based on the color of your skin. You embody greatness beyond your full understanding of who you are. You are the epitome of success despite the many traps meant to oppress you as a black man. The weight of the world may feel like it's on your shoulders, but always remember you exemplify the courage and heart of your ancestors.

I Love You.

~ Tiriq

"You will sit under trees that you didn't have to plant."

Letters of LOVE from
RUBEN STEWART III

"Those who have the biggest impact in the world are the least controlled by it" ~ KB

Dear Young King,

Many things in life may require an explanation so do not ever be afraid to ask for directions. The world may seem tough, but God gave you everything you need to succeed. When I see you, I see the future and don't ever let them tell you anything different. Throughout our history, there are examples of what we can accomplish when we work together. So when the burden gets too heavy, always ask for help, somethings are not meant for us to carry alone.

Lean on your brothers as you walk through life, as we are here to help you in every way possible. Use these words to push you when times get hard, to pull you up when you need a hand, and to uplift you when you are feeling down. We love you and are dedicating our lives to contribute to your success. I hope these words can bring light to your day when the sky seems grey. Stay inspired and always think positive.

I Love You,

~ Ruben

"Some people want it to happen, some wish it would happen, others make it happen." ~ Michael Jordan

Dear Young King,

You are stronger than you may know. There is only one thing in this world that can hold you back and that one thing is you. Your mind is full of endless possibilities, so free your mind from all the things you think you cannot do and start to think of all the things you can do. There will always be people who say you cannot do it, but never lose sight of that light that burns inside you, which says you can.

I want you to build your version of success, and once you do, you will see that the world is yours. Set your goals and chase them and never settle for less than YOUR BEST. These are some of the best examples of men who did not let their neighborhood or where they were raised stop them from making their dreams come true. People like LeBron James, Barack Obama, and Jay-z. All of these men faced challenges just like yours daily, but because of the belief they had in themselves, those obstacles did not keep them down.

Don't ever be afraid of failure, that is just life's way of teaching you a lesson, so learn from them. I believe in you even when you feel like no one is listening or that no one sees you. I will never stop cheering for your success. So let's make it happen.

I Love You,

~ Ruben

"God took away my Sight, so I could see."
~ Ruben Stewart III

Dear Young King,

Some days you may feel like life is cheating you. Believe me when I say I know exactly how you feel. This is not something I share often, but my love for you won't allow me to hide my truth. I was born with a rare eye disease called Retinitis Pigmentosa, don't worry I can barely say it. This disease causes me to lose my vision over time.

As a kid, it wreaked havoc on my life. It stopped me from playing sports and my performance in school suffered due to me not being able to see the board. As I grew older, I began to believe that what I have always seen as my curse, had become my gift. Due to my low vision, I am forced to pay super close attention to my surroundings.

This forces me to see every move a person might make before they make it in order not to bump into them or make a mistake. I share my secret with you because I want you to use my story as motivation. You can always turn your negatives into positives. Even with my disability, I have managed to complete most of my goals thus far.

You have all of the tools you need to be everything you ever wanted to be. Use my story and the stories of others to give you a push in the right direction when you are feeling down. God will never put anything on your plate that you cannot handle. You are a Young King and I cannot wait to see what you do next.

I Love You,

~ Ruben

"You have to be tough to be blessed."
~ Bishop T.D. Jakes

Dear Young King,

There may be many challenges throughout your day, but you can never let fear stop you from overcoming them. I want you to have courage, in knowing that when you walk out that door you are not alone. There are a lot of people rooting for you. We are putting together a large group of men who have already walked down a path similar to yours, our numbers grow daily.

We are and will always have your back. Take courage in knowing that you have a team behind you whether you see them or not. Change can sometimes be scary, but with change comes growth and growth is amazing. The biggest part of life is growth. You will begin to see the world from a different view.

As a young man, life will begin to move faster at this point in your life. Always stay true to who you are even when doing so becomes frustrating. You are smart and brave and can do all you set out to do. Not only do I believe in you, but all the men who came together to write this book

believe in you as well. Have faith and trust your instincts.
Have an awesome day!

I Love You,

~ Ruben

"As we walk through life we will be remembered most for our Actions and Deeds." ~ Ruben Stewart III

Dear Young King,

You were born to be a leader, but as a young man, you have to follow before you get your chance to lead. The key is knowing who to follow and who not to. Some leaders are just a good speech, while others use those words to guide their actions. Like most things in life, leadership has to be earned. It is not given to the faster, the tallest, or even to the smartest.

It's earned through our actions and deeds. In the world of social media, it can become difficult to tell the difference. A truthful man knows only liars are afraid of the truth, however, let your word be your bond and your actions be the proof.

So always follow the truth. Young King, I am addressing you as if you were my nephew, brother, or son because you are a part of my family and I love and accept you just the way you are. The knowledge we have shared with you in this book is meant to motivate and inspire.

Although I am well aware that some of it may be difficult for you to understand, I guarantee that it will be essential to your growth as a man. I encourage you to ask as many questions as necessary for you to absorb it. I want to say congratulations on all of your future successes. Last but not least, I want to say don't forget to put on your crown before you walk out of that door.

I Love You,

~ Ruben

"You can't wear a crown with your head down, stand tall and confident."

Letters of LOVE from

TONY CHATMAN

"You can kill the dreamer, but you can't kill the dream."

~ Dr. Martin Luther King Jr.

Little brother, there will be tons of people telling you that you can't do it. Question them. Ask them, "Why do you believe that?" Most of the time it's because they are fearful themselves. They didn't achieve their dreams and they think you can't. Your dreams will not wait for you, nor should others influence them. Keep your nose to the grindstone and all the things you believe in will come true!

I love you,

~ Tony

*"My thing is that I don't give no person that much power
over my path that I am walking. Not one person can make
or break what I'm doing, except me or God."*

~ Nipsey Hussle

Young King,

*I remember when I was in your shoes. But for me, I
was the little brother and a big brother. On one side, I had
a big brother that I adored and wanted to be like. Then, on
the other hand, I was the big brother that had a pair of eyes
on me. Throughout my life, I started to realize that the path
that my older brother walked, was not the path that I
wanted to walk. Not saying his path was the wrong path,
but it wasn't my path.*

*As I thought about how I envisioned my future, I knew
it was supposed to be different. We are all born different.
This was something that I wanted to show my little brother
as early as possible. No matter how much you look up to
someone, never forget that your path still needs to be walked.
Your steps can only be walked by you.*

I love you,

~ Tony

"I have learned that success is to be measured not so much by the position that one has reached in life as by the obstacles which he has had to overcome while trying to succeed."

~ Booker T. Washington

Young King,

Listen, life isn't going to go your way. There will be bumps, potholes, and all kinds of obstacles in your way. Shit, there will be hills as high as the clouds and valleys as deep as the sea. But guess what, don't let any of that stop you. These trials and tribulations will create a version of you that only you can allow. I promise you that if you look deep within yourself and see these as speed bumps and lessons, you'll be the greatest form of yourself. DON'T LET NOTHING STOP YOU.

I love you,

~ Tony

"It's the one thing you can control. You are responsible for how people remember you, or don't. So don't take it lightly."

~ Kobe Bryant

Young King,

I want you to look at yourself and think, "When I am 20 years older than I am now, what will this version of myself today, think of me?" That's a deep question, I know. But the steps that I am taking now are so that you will never have to go through the things that my forefathers and I had to go through. I love you enough to endure the pain and struggle now so you won't have to. Right now, I want you to think about every step you take, every move you make from this day forward. It directly affects your future.

Every day that passes, try to carve a little bit of the stone that you see as yourself in the future. As your days begin to pass, guess what? No one cares if you do or don't do anything. Continue striving to be the best version of you. Remember, The greats never think about being mediocre?

I love you,

~ Tony

*"I'd rather be happy being, myself than sad trying
to please everyone else." ~ J. Cole*

Young King,

*I want you to know that you're enough. I know I do
not tell you enough, but you are. Everything about you is
amazing; from your chocolate skin, your thick nappy hair,
your wide nose, your thick lips, that natural muscle
definition that you have, you are a beautiful king. Don't let
anyone tell you any different. Keep dreaming so big that
people think you are crazy. Follow your beliefs and stay
positive. Even when you feel like the world is on your
shoulders, don't be so quick to give up.*

*Endure that battle and learn from it. Let your strong
spirit and radiant smile light up this world. You have the
power to let your positive energy shine, light bright in this
dark world. Be strong not just for you but for the other
Kings around you. Let them know that they can lean on you
when they are in a time of need.*

*Stay positive and never let someone's negativity have a
hold on you. Remember that the positive vibrations that you
provide will not allow the negative ones in. You can't afford*

that setback. Keep moving forward and believe that everything that you need to do, can and will be done.

It's all up to you King.

I love you,

~ Tony

"We LOVE you!"

Letters of LOVE from

CHRISTIAN RAGLAND

"Information is out there, education is the discipline
to acquire it" ~ Carter G. Woodson

Dear Young Future Leader,

Two types of people exist. The first are those who do enough just to get by and the second are those who go above and beyond what is expected. Please hear me when I say that I made a successful living doing the extra things that the others around me did not want to do. Always go above and beyond what is expected of you. Yes, this may make your days longer, your work harder and you may not see the immediate impact of your effort, but you will reap the rewards sooner than you think.

Do not surround yourself with people who are okay with doing the bare minimum. Matter of fact, identify those individuals who are content with being average and be mindful. This will help you clean your circle of influence and power. Learn to love going the extra mile in everything that you do because that is where your character is built. Success and opportunities come to those who built their character to sustain success. Do not overwork yourself, but again learn how to use that work ethic to your advantage.

I Love You,
~ Christian

"I have learned some of my greatest lessons helping
the wrong people!" ~ Christian D. Ragland

Dear Young Future Leader,

You will find out very early on that people will look to you for help in many ways! With that being said, please remember that not everyone who asks for help needs your help. Remember that not every problem is your assignment. Some people will depend on your willingness to disguise their laziness. Do not burn yourself out helping the wrong people!

Do not get me wrong, you will stand on the shoulders of giants who have directly and indirectly helped you already, but use wisdom. There will be people looking for the easy way out while you take the long and hard way to help them. This is not something that you would want to become your "Normal"! Your biggest frustration could be people who ask for help but are not prepared to receive what they are asking you for.

Please trust me and learn this lesson now; not everyone is going to receive your help and that is okay. Self-care is making sure that you are stable and healthy enough to help the right people who are assigned to your life. Just stay humble and listen to the people who truly care about you.

I Love You,

~ Christian

EPILOGUE

A large portion of our children in America especially in the African American community doesn't make it out alive when they are ignored by the very people who should be helping them build their self-esteem and loving on them. In the American Journal of Orthopsychiatry, an article titled "Boys do(n't) cry: Addressing the unmet mental health needs of African American boys." Written by Dr. Michael Lindsay (Executive director of the NYU McSilver Institute) it stated that "African American communities are lacking safe places for black boys to express and release their emotions and they also lack support groups as well, which all contribute to the decisions of taking matters into their own hands and ending their lives prematurely."

So I want you to do me a favor and ask yourself, "Have I turned my empathy button off?" Because I can guarantee that many of you have. If that's you, I'm not asking you to raise your hand but I am asking you to turn it back on. By creating an atmosphere of love and communication, psychologically we can positively shape the minds of our black youth and help them build their self-esteem, provide them with a sense of safety, and also save their lives.

ACKNOWLEDGMENT

Thank you to Alan Laws Jr, Alex Speaks, Christian Ragland, Darrell Edmonds, Les Squair Jr, Michael Forest, Ricardo Belgrave, Ruben Stewart III, Tiriq Callaway, Tony Chatman, Tyrell Lewis, Tywane Russell. Thank you for contributing your experiences, wisdom, and love for this movement. I believe that the letters that you all have shared will encourage, inspire, and shift the perspective of countless black boys for years to come. With this book, we have an opportunity to change lives and even save the lives of our black boys.

RESOURCES

Black Mental Health Alliance
https://blackmentalhealth.com

Boris Lawrence Henson Foundation
https://borislhensonfoundation.org

12 books on behavioral health written by black people
https://blackmentalhealth.com/12-books-on-behavioral-
health-written-by-black-people/

Training Programs
https://blackmentalhealth.com/the-national-institute-for-
maximal-human-development/

Directory of Black Psychologists
https://blackmentalhealth.com/black-psychiatrists/

Suicide: Facts, Signs, and Intervention
https://blackmentalhealth.com/12-books-on-behavioral-
health-written-by-black-people/

National Suicide Prevention Hotline
(1-800-273-8255)

Made in the USA
Coppell, TX
27 July 2021